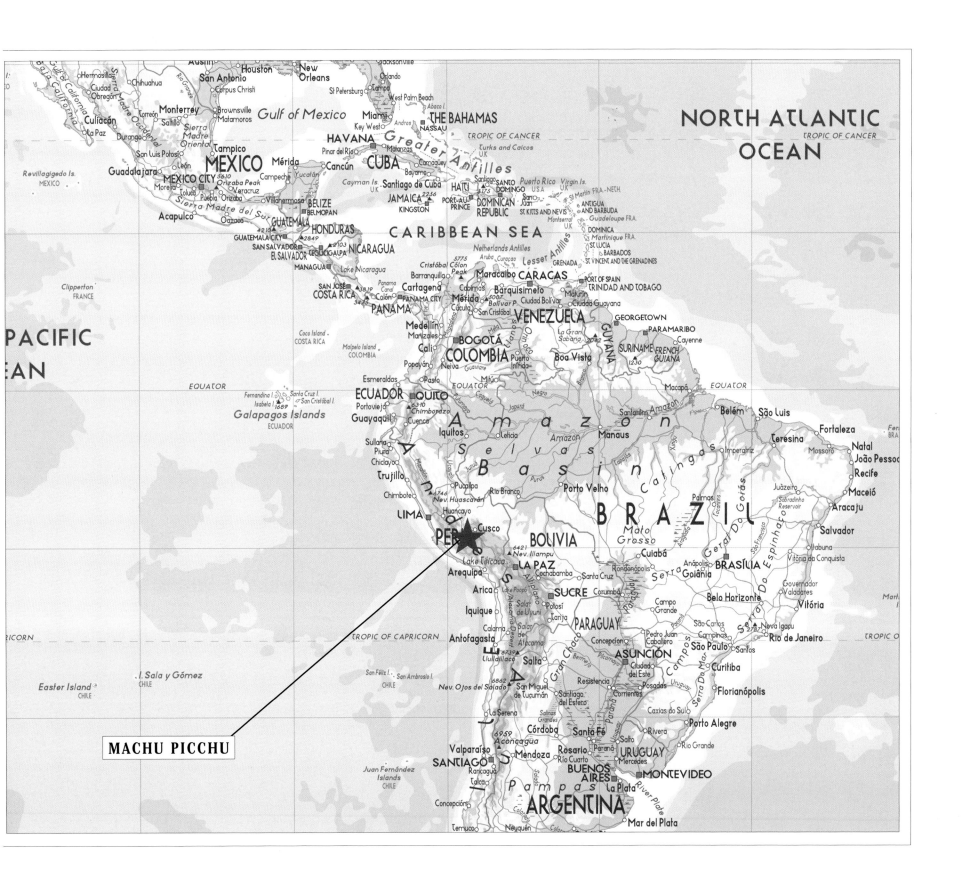

MACHU PICCHU

Published by Creative Education
123 South Broad Street
Mankato, Minnesota 56001

Creative Education is an imprint of The Creative Company.

Designed by Stephanie Blumenthal
Production design by The Design Lab
Art direction by Rita Marshall

Photographs by Corbis (Tom Bean, Bettmann, Gary Braasch, Michael & Patricia Fogden,
Werner Forman, Darell Gulin, John Van Hasselt, Historical Picture Archive, Dave G.
Houser, Wolfgang Kaehler, Lake County Museum, Charles & Josette Lenars, Craig Lovell,
Renee Lynn, Franklin McMahon, Pilar Olivares, Forestier Patrick, Reuters, Bill Ross, Galen Rowell,
Kevin Schafer, Leonard de Selva, Alex Steedman, Keren Su, Pablo Corral Vega, Brian A. Vikander,
Alison Wright), Getty Images (Taxi), North Wind Picture Archives (9)

Printed in the United States of America

Library of Congress Cataloging-in-Publication Data

Peterson, Sheryl.
Machu Picchu / by Sheryl Peterson.
p. cm. — (Ancient wonders of the world)
Includes index.
ISBN 1-58341-357-X
1. Machu Picchu Site (Peru)—Juvenile literature. 2. Incas—History—Juvenile
literature. 3. Inca architecture—Juvenile literature. 4. Peru—Antiquities—Juvenile literature. I. Title. II. Series.

F3429.1.M3P48 2005   985'.37—dc22   2004055269

First edition

2 4 6 8 9 7 5 3 1

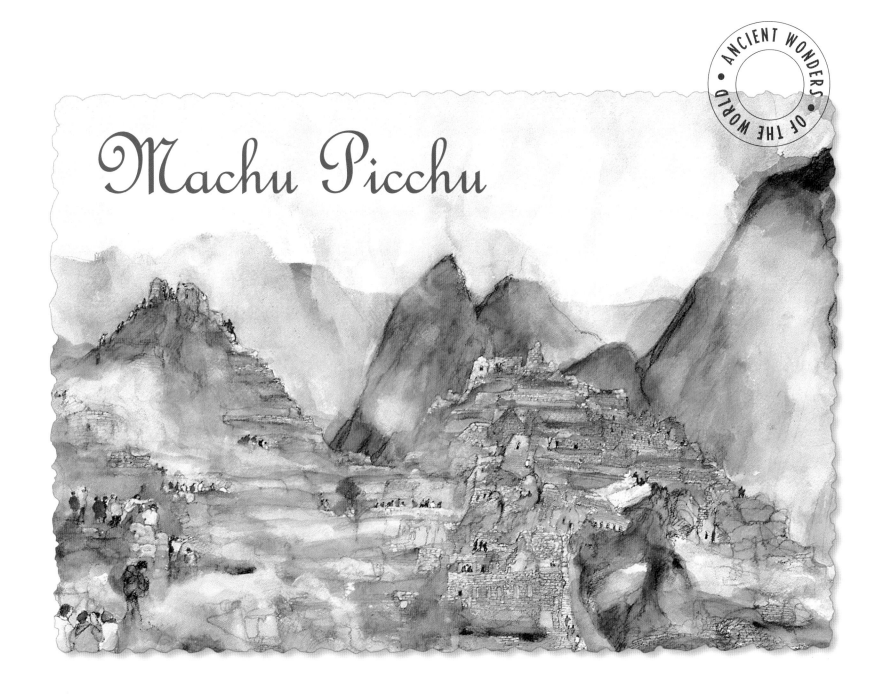

Machu Picchu

SHERYL PETERSON

CREATIVE EDUCATION

MACHU PICCHU

Concealed in the cloud-shrouded Andes mountains, with only alpacas and other animals to roam its lonely terrain, the ancient city of Machu Picchu remained lost for almost 400 years.

Glaciered, snow-capped mountains tower overhead. The roaring Urubamba River snakes along its triangular course below. Between the two, high on a **granite** ridge, rests Machu Picchu, the mysterious Inca city invisible from below. Ancient stone buildings, abandoned and hidden for more than three centuries, still stand intact, minus only their **thatched** roofs. Who lived there? Why and how was this city built in such an impossible place? Although many answers have been unearthed in the last 100 years, there remains an air of mystery about this secret city in the clouds.

When a local peasant talked of ruins high up in the Andes mountains, Hiram Bingham paid the man one Peruvian silver dollar (50 cents U.S.) to be his guide. The farmer grew tired, however, and ultimately an 11-year-old boy named Pablito Alverez led Bingham to the hidden city of Machu Picchu.

THE INCA EMPIRE

In the late 1400s, about the time Christopher Columbus arrived in America, there came to power a race of Indians called the Incas. This society dwelled on the western slope of the Andes mountains in what is now the South American country of Peru and became a remarkably skilled and organized civilization.

The Incas were master **architects** and road builders. Without the benefit of the wheel, they built a vast and sophisticated system of stone roads unlike any of their time, leading from the sea to the mountaintops. The Incas had no horses, but trained messengers running in relays could cover as much as 250 miles (400 km) per day and deliver news quickly to distant areas.

Expertly woven rope bridges, made by braiding vines together, stretched across river canyons for easy passage.

Inca society was ruled by a god-like, all-powerful ruler called the Inca. Beneath him were the royal family, several levels of nobles and priests, and finally the common people, comprised mainly of craftsmen and farmers. People's lives were strictly controlled, but the Inca government made sure they had what they needed to work and live. At the height of its glory in the 15th century, the Inca empire extended the length of the South American coast from Ecuador to Chile.

Inca religion was centered on worship of the sun. The Inca ruler was worshipped as a

The main god of the Incas was the sun god, Inti. He was the giver and protector of life, and he brought people warmth and light. When the sun dropped into the ocean each evening at sunset, the Inca people were afraid that their god might not be able to swim under the earth and reappear the next morning in the east.

From the bank of the fast-moving Urubamba River, the bus road (opposite) leading to Machu Picchu rises through 13 hairpin turns.

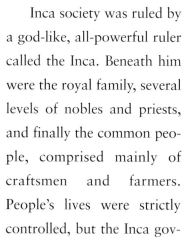

6

The Incas ate mostly corn, guinea pigs, and a high-protein grain called quinoa. They also grew more than 200 kinds of potatoes. In fact, the potato was so important to the Incas that they used the length of time it took to boil one as a way of measuring time.

Innovations such as the quipa (below) and terraced fields (right) helped Inca cities such as Cusco (opposite) flourish.

god descended from the sun god, Inti. People also offered prayers to Mother Earth, the sea, and the moon. Ancestors were worshipped as helpful spirits who acted as links between the living and the gods.

The Inca population grew to more than 10 million people. Although they had no alphabet or written language, the Incas developed a numerical device called a *quipa,* which used knots and colored strings as counting units. The device kept accurate records of population data and agricultural inventories, but it could be read only by skilled interpreters.

Agriculture was tough business in the Andes due to the steep pitch of the landscape. To make planting easier, the Incas carved up the mountains into **terraced** farmlands. Their efforts were so successful that in 1500, more land was in cultivation in the Andean highlands than there is today. Crops such as beans and corn were planted at different elevations to create new varieties.

Of all the native peoples of the Americas, the Incas were the most brilliant

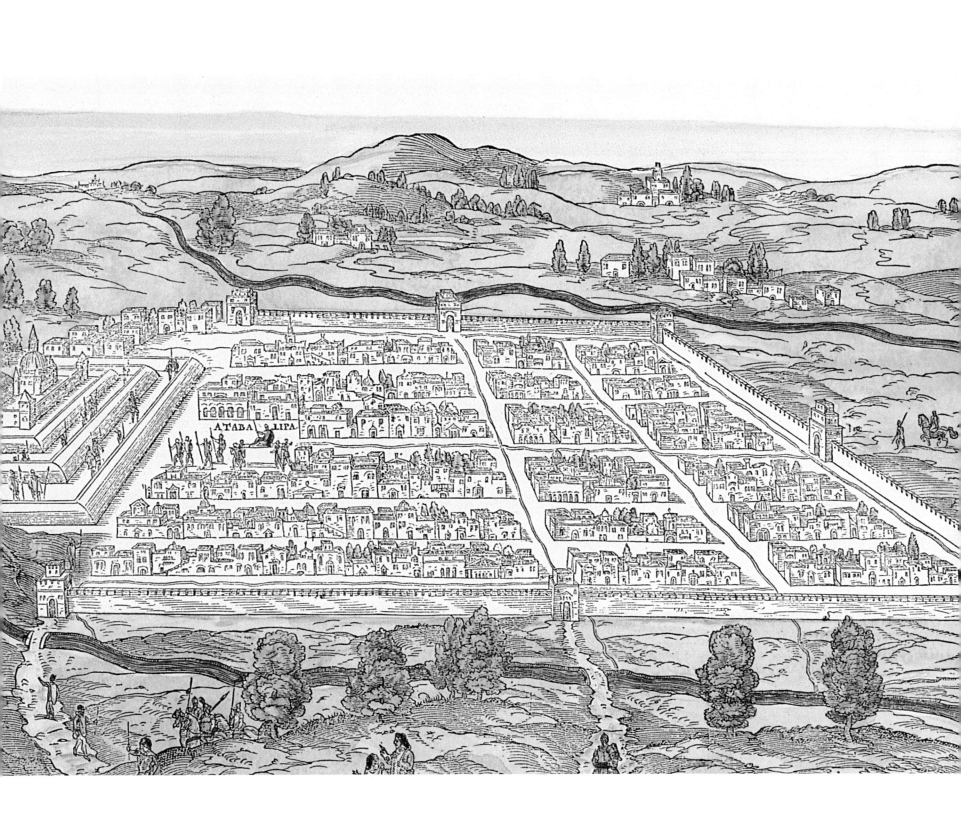

"Work" was the watchword of the Inca empire, and its ritual salute was its slogan: *Manan sua, manna lluella, manna quella* ("Do not steal, do not kill, do not be lazy"). Inca men could pay their taxes by hauling huge stones for the building of Machu Picchu.

engineers. Their engineering skill was put to use between 1460 and 1470, when the great Inca ruler Pachacuti oversaw construction of an imperial terraced city high in the mountains. The city, named Machu Picchu, sat like a saddle between two giant mountain peaks 8,040 feet (2,450 m) above the Urubamba River.

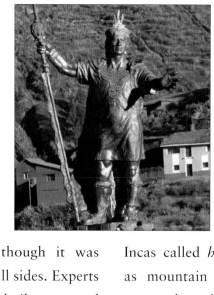

Contrary to early guesses by historians, Machu Picchu was not designed as a military fortress, even though it was defended by sheer cliffs on all sides. Experts now agree that the city was built as a royal retreat and sacred ceremonial center.

Machu Picchu lay at a lower, warmer altitude than the lofty Inca capital of Cusco, and therefore provided milder weather.

At Machu Picchu's secluded location, some 75 miles (120 km) northwest of Cusco, the Incas made astronomical observations, charted the sun's path across the sky, and made sacrifices to Inti for good harvests. It was a sanctuary surrounded by what the Incas called *huacas*, natural features such as mountain peaks and life-giving river water that the Incas believed possessed supernatural powers.

The vast Inca empire included not only Machu Picchu, which was constructed under the guidance of Pachacuti (opposite), but also the settlement of Huinay Huayna (top). In addition to constructing buildings, the skilled Incas also built a massive stone calendar (bottom) to track days and seasons.

AN ARCHITECTURAL MIRACLE

Primitive tools (below) were used to cut all of the stones that make up the houses, temples, and other buildings of the city. Even the trapezoidal doorways (right) were constructed from stones of various shapes and sizes. Although some stones had as many as 30 corners, they all fit together perfectly.

It would have required a great amount of ingenuity and a considerable army of laborers to move all of the massive stones into place and build the more than 200 structures that made up the city of Machu Picchu. Stones were cut so precisely that there was no need for mortar; not even a knife blade could fit between the white granite layers. It is still not clear how the workers moved the huge boulders from the riverbed quarry so far below, cut them with only stone hammers, and then polished them so expertly with sand.

Cascading down the mountain from the city are stone-walled ter-races that had two functions: to grow crops and to limit **erosion** caused by rain. Constant showers and high, ever-present **humidity** served as natural irrigation for crops. In the terraced plots, farmers grew corn, potatoes, and medicinal herbs for the more than 1,000 nobles and workers who lived in the city.

Machu Picchu covers five square miles (13 sq km) and is U-shaped. It is edged with terraces and an inner wall, which would have helped guard the city from invaders. In the southern section are houses and work-shops built around central courtyards and connected by narrow alleys. In the days of the Incas, the stone homes had thatched roofs and

Machu Picchu's unusual layout is best seen from a mountain peak above the city. Some say the city is shaped like a hummingbird, a bird that was special to the Incas. Others have offered the wild idea that it may have been a landing spot for visitors from another planet.

Stone fragments that were chipped away to shape the structures in Machu Picchu were "recycled" and put to good use elsewhere. Rock chips were layered in the courtyards to provide drainage and to stabilize the ground. Sixty percent of the construction at Machu Picchu lies in underground foundations—an impressive feat of engineering.

trapezoidal windows. Stairways were cleverly carved out of huge blocks of stone. Homes had raised stone platforms for sleeping, niches carved in the walls for storage, and stone pegs on which to hang clothing.

In the city's northern sector are religious shrines. One of the most significant is the Temple of the Sun, which has a semicircular shape and is built on a natural rock formation. The temple is considered by astronomers to be a solar observatory and features a window through which the rays of the June **solstice** sunrise enter and fall parallel to a line carved into a sacred rock.

Another unique creation found in the city's northern sector is the Intihuatana stone, which was sculpted from a natural rock pyramid. In the Incas' Quechua language, *Intihuatana* means "the hitching post of the sun." It is a six-foot (1.8 m), four-sided pillar that serves as a natural sundial. It is believed that the Incas built the Intihuatana for priests who tried to capture the power of the sun and bind it to the rock. The post enabled the Incas to accurately determine the time of day, calendar days and weeks, and agricultural planting times.

Machu Picchu is filled with engineering marvels. Stone stairways flank a series of fountains (opposite) that could handle up to 26 gallons (100 l) of water a minute. The round Temple of the Sun features the most perfect stonework in the city. The 35-foot-wide (10.5 m) temple was used for the Inca celebration of Inti-raymi *during the winter solstice.*

Orchids (right), butterflies (below and opposite bottom left), llamas (opposite top left), and parrots (opposite top right) thrive near Machu Picchu. The Incas made use of their natural surroundings by harnessing the power of a nearby spring to supply water to the city's fountains (opposite bottom right).

Water is critical to any community, and the founders of Machu Picchu cleverly built five-inch-wide (12 cm) rock canals to distribute water from a natural mountain spring nearby. The water flowed down a series of 16 fountains, starting at the Royal Residence (home to the Inca ruler and his family) and bubbling alongside the 100 stairways and 3,000 steps in the urban sector.

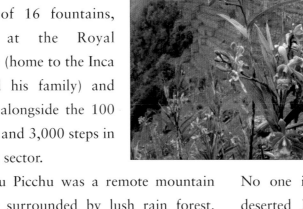

Machu Picchu was a remote mountain hideaway surrounded by lush rain forest. Exotic orchids peeked out of ferns, multicolored parrots, macaws, and butterflies

flew overhead, lizards basked in the sun, and llamas roamed the steep landscape. Inca citizens lived in this serene, sacred spot for more than 100 years.

In about 1532, Spanish explorer Francisco Pizarro and his army of conquistadors, or soldiers, marched into Peru in search of fabled Inca riches. With their advanced armor and weapons, they quickly conquered the Inca empire. No one is certain when the Inca people deserted Machu Picchu, but there is no evidence that the Spaniards ever found the ceremonial city.

1 9

Llamas, alpacas, and vicuñas were very important animals to the Incas. Alpacas were herded in mountain pastures, and their wool was used for clothing. The wild vicuñas were captured, shorn of their fine wool, and then released. Llamas were sometimes killed for meat but were mostly used as pack animals.

UNCOVERING THE SLEEPING BEAUTY

Hiram Bingham (1875–1956) was born in Honolulu, Hawaii, the son and grandson of **missionaries**. He graduated from Yale University in 1898. After his explorations in South America, Bingham went on to become Connecticut's lieutenant governor, governor, and a United States senator.

With no written records to document its existence, Machu Picchu slept under the vines and moss-hung trees for almost four centuries. While the rest of the Inca empire was changed forever by Spanish influence, the hidden city stayed intact.

On July 24, 1911, a Yale University professor and **archaeologist** named Hiram Bingham was in Peru searching for the ancestral origin of the Inca people. Bingham and his team hiked up a new mule road that had just been cleared. While the rest of the team set up camp, Bingham continued on alone, inspired by the stories of local peasants who reported seeing ruins higher up in the mountains.

When Bingham first laid eyes on Machu Picchu, he was stunned by its majesty, evident even under the layers of moss and dense vegetation. After retrieving his team to begin the uncovering process, Bingham wrote excitedly in his journal, "I know of no other place in the world which can compare with it. What could this place be?"

Bingham returned to Peru a year later with a group financed by the National Geographic Society to explore Machu Picchu further. He hired local Indians to cut down trees and bushes, burn branches, and clean the walls of the ancient buildings. Bingham expected to discover treasures of gold left behind, but he

Hiram Bingham's (opposite) discovery of Machu Picchu sparked an interest in archaeological study in the Andes and throughout South America. Machu Picchu means "old peak" in the Incas' Quechua language, while the name of the peak behind the city, Huayna Picchu (left), means "new peak."

Up to 2,000 people from around the world visit Machu Picchu every day, making it one of South America's top tourist destinations. Although no gold was found there, items such as wooden drinking cups and silver figurines (below) survive from the Inca era.

found only pottery, bronze jewelry, and stone tools. The royal residents, fearful they would never return, must have packed up all of their prized possessions when they abandoned the city.

Since Bingham's incredible discovery unveiled Machu Picchu to the world, many archeologists have traveled to the secluded city. Every year, more than 300,000 adventurous tourists also visit Machu Picchu. Not long ago, visitors could climb the mountains to the ruins on their own, but the resulting damage to the trails and environment led to a crackdown by the Peruvian government. Since 2001, new regulations have required that hikers be accompanied by a licensed tour guide. Today, there are more than 100 licensed tour operators in the area, complete with guides, porters, and cooks.

Many peasants in the hills around Machu Picchu still farm, but some have become porters for visitors. Local women sell rugs and butterfly collections at train stations in nearby cities such as Aguas Calientes. Area children pose for pictures and run after buses to catch tossed coins. The ancient Inca roads, once swept clean daily for the empire's runners, are at times now crowded with camera-carrying tourists.

2 2

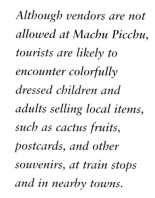

Although vendors are not allowed at Machu Picchu, tourists are likely to encounter colorfully dressed children and adults selling local items, such as cactus fruits, postcards, and other souvenirs, at train stops and in nearby towns.

With its beautiful carvings and **subterranean** passageways, the Temple of the Condor is one of the most fascinating temples in Machu Picchu. Hiram Bingham thought that important **mummies** may have been displayed there.

Condors, such as the one carved into the temple floor at Machu Picchu (right), are now an endangered species. Llamas (opposite), on the other hand, continue to frequent the site.

Since Machu Picchu has become so popular with tourists, Peruvian officials have begun developing Choquequirao, an area of ruins called the "Cradle of Gold" buried in the jungle 50 miles (80 km) to the south. Experts believe Choquequirao may have been a refuge for rebel Incas after the collapse of their civilization.

In recent years, a struggle has developed between

people who want to best preserve Machu Picchu and those who want to better open it up for tourism. One plan involves building a cable car line to carry visitors up to the ancient ruins. Many environmentalists and

archaeologists—who already worry about the Sanctuary Lodge hotel built right next to the city—are opposed to the plan, which would likely double the daily tourist count.

A majestic mountaintop island in a sea of green jungle and craggy rocks, Machu Picchu is a city unlike any other on Earth. Since revealing itself to the world almost a century ago, it has shared secrets about an ancient culture and left countless visitors in awe. Provided that people continue to respect and protect this masterpiece in the clouds, Machu Picchu will endure as long as the mountains themselves.

SEEING THE WONDER

The outdoor enthusiast may enjoy camping along the 25-mile-long (40 km), high-altitude Inca Trail to Machu Picchu. Reservations must be made in advance, though, since the Peruvian government limits the number of people on the trail to 500 a day, including the required guides.

Although Machu Picchu is still shrouded in mystery to much of the world, thousands of adventurers and sightseers flock to Peru's primary tourist attraction every year. Most visitors get there by flying to Lima, Peru, and then taking a plane or bus to Cusco, the gateway to the historic city.

From Cusco, fit and adventurous tourists might embark on a hiking trip to Machu Picchu with a guide, camping at night and taking in some stunning scenic lookouts. Those interested in a more leisurely trip up the mountain may hop on a train. There are several train options of different cost and luxury levels; a trip on the most expensive, the *Hiram Bingham*, includes a three-course brunch and dinner. The railroad ends in Aguas Calientes, a village known for its hot springs. From there, travelers are taken by bus to Machu Picchu.

Visitors can find a number of moderately priced hotels in Aguas Calientes. For more luxurious accommodations, tourists who can afford it might consider staying at the $500-a-night Machu Picchu

27

Many tourists travel to the ancient city by way of modern transportation. A train ride through the mountains provides beautiful views of valleys, snow-capped peaks, and the rushing Urubamba River. After a day of sightseeing at Machu Picchu, several hotels are available in nearby cities.

More than 400 colorful bird species can be seen around Machu Picchu. This includes the brilliant red cock-of-the-rock and the trilling tapaculo, a small bird that sneaks around like a mouse and sometimes surprises people with its loud song.

Birds such as the great blue heron (right) and Inca tern (below) add to the natural beauty of Machu Picchu.

Sanctuary Lodge. Guests at this ritzy hotel may wander the historic site with the ever-present llamas after the crowds have left for the day.

Foreign tourists need a passport to enter Peru and should receive the necessary **inoculations** before their trip. Visitors to Machu Picchu are encouraged to drink lots of bottled water, take frequent rest breaks, and eat small snacks often—all of which help a person's body adjust to the high mountain altitude. The change in altitude can give some people nausea, headaches, and **vertigo**.

The best time to visit Machu Picchu is from May to September, when the weather is dry and warm and the wild orchids are in bloom. The temperature at the mountain city averages about 60 °F (16 °C) year-round, so packing some warm clothing is a good idea. Comfortable shoes are also a must for handling the rocky terrain. Visitors are encouraged to check the news for up-to-date travel information. In April 2004, heavy rains caused a huge mudslide near Machu Picchu, and hundreds of visitors had to be evacuated by helicopter.

28

MACHU  PICCHU

QUICK FACTS

Location: Peru; about 75 miles (120 km) northwest of the city of Cusco

Age: ~ 550 years

Elevation: 8,040 feet (2,450 m) above sea level

Area covered: Five square miles (13 sq km)

Composition: 200 white granite buildings

Builders: Inca Indian laborers under Inca ruler Pachacuti

Time occupied: ~ 100 years

First foreigner to view: American archaeologist Hiram Bingham (July 24, 1911)

Geographic setting: Mountains

Visitors per year: More than 300,000

Native plant life: Includes vines, bamboo, tree ferns, rock roses, begonias, and more than 90 species of wild orchids

Native animal life: Includes llamas, alpacas, vicuñas, spectacled bears, lizards, and snakes; numerous tropical birds such as hummingbirds, falcons, hawks, cuckoos, parrots, tanagers, macaws, and herons

Other Name: Old Mountain

GLOSSARY

archaeologist—scientist who learns about the past by digging up and studying old structures or objects

architects—people who design buildings and other structures and oversee their construction

engineers—people skilled at designing buildings or public works

erosion—the gradual wearing away of something by wind and water

granite—a very hard kind of rock produced by intense heat underground

humidity—water vapor in the air; a rain forest has high humidity, making the air feel damp

inoculations—medicinal shots given to people to prevent them from getting certain diseases

missionaries—people who go to a foreign country to spread religion or do charity work

mummies—dead bodies that are dried and wrapped in linen bandages in an ancient preservation technique

solstice—the time when the sun is farthest from Earth's equator (about June 21 and December 22)

subterranean—hidden below ground

terraced—built in a series of levels rising one above the other; used to describe land used for growing crops

thatched—covered with natural materials such as straw, leaves, or rushes

trapezoidal—describing a four-sided shape that has two sides parallel and two sides uneven

vertigo—a condition in which a person becomes dizzy and feels as if things are spinning

Andes mountains 5, 6

Bingham, Hiram 5, 20, 22, 24, 30

climate 10, 14, 28

Columbus, Christopher 6

farming 8, 14, 16, 22

Inca

  empire 6, 10, 18, 20, 24

  population 8

  religion 6, 8, 10, 16

  roads 6, 22

  rulers 6, 8, 10, 18, 30

Inti 6, 8, 10

Intihuatana stone 16

Machu Picchu

  abandonment 18, 22

  age 30

  buildings 4, 14, 16, 18, 30

  construction 10, 14, 16, 30

  discovery 5, 20, 22

  geographical location 4, 10, 30

  layout 14, 16, 18

  purpose 10

  size 14, 30

mummies 24, 30

National Geographic Society 20

Peru 6, 10, 20, 22, 24, 26, 30

  Aguas Calientes 22, 26

  Choquequirao 24

  Cusco 10, 26, 30

  Lima 26

Pizarro, Francisco 18

plant life 8, 14, 18, 28, 30

quipa 8

Sanctuary Lodge 24, 26, 28

temples 16, 24

  Temple of the Condor 24

  Temple of the Sun 16

tourism 22, 24, 26, 28, 30

  opposition 24

Urubamba River 4, 10

water 14, 18

wildlife 18, 19, 28, 30

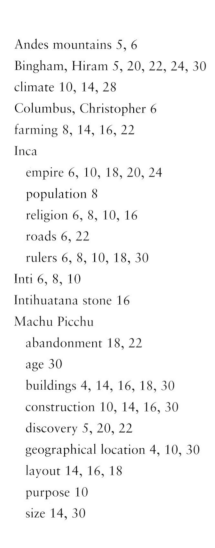